W9-BRI-326

This Is a Let's-Read-and-Find-Out Science Book®

EARTHQUAKES

by Franklyn M. Branley   illustrated by Richard Rosenblum

Thomas Y. Crowell   New York

The *Let's-Read-and-Find-Out Science Book* series was originated by Dr. Franklyn M. Branley, Astronomer Emeritus and former Chairman of the American Museum–Hayden Planetarium, and was formerly co-edited by him and Dr. Roma Gans, Professor Emeritus of Childhood Education, Teachers College, Columbia University. For a complete catalog of Let's-Read-and-Find-Out Science Books, write to Thomas Y. Crowell Junior Books, Harper & Row, Publishers, Inc., 10 East 53rd Street, New York, NY 10022.

Let's-Read-and-Find-Out Science Book is a registered
trademark of Harper & Row, Publishers, Inc.
Earthquakes
Text copyright © 1990 by Franklyn M. Branley
Illustrations copyright © 1990 by Richard Rosenblum

1 2 3 4 5 6 7 8 9 10

First Edition

Library of Congress Cataloging-in-Publication Data
Branley, Franklyn Mansfield, 1915–
    Earthquakes / by Franklyn M. Branley ; illustrated by Richard
Rosenblum.
        p.   cm. — (A Let's-read-and-find-out science book)
    Summary: Discusses why earthquakes happen, what their sometimes
devastating effects can be, where the danger zones are, and what
measures people can take to safeguard themselves.
        ISBN 0-690-04661-8 : $. — ISBN 0-690-04663-4 (lib. bdg.) : $

    1. Earthquakes—Juvenile literature. [1. Earthquakes.]
I. Rosenblum, Richard, ill.   II. Title.   III. Series.
QE521.3.B72 1990   89-35424
551.2′2—dc20   CIP
                                                 AC

EARTHQUAKES

Parts of the Earth are always moving. That's hard to believe, but they are. The movements are so small and so slow, we usually cannot feel them.

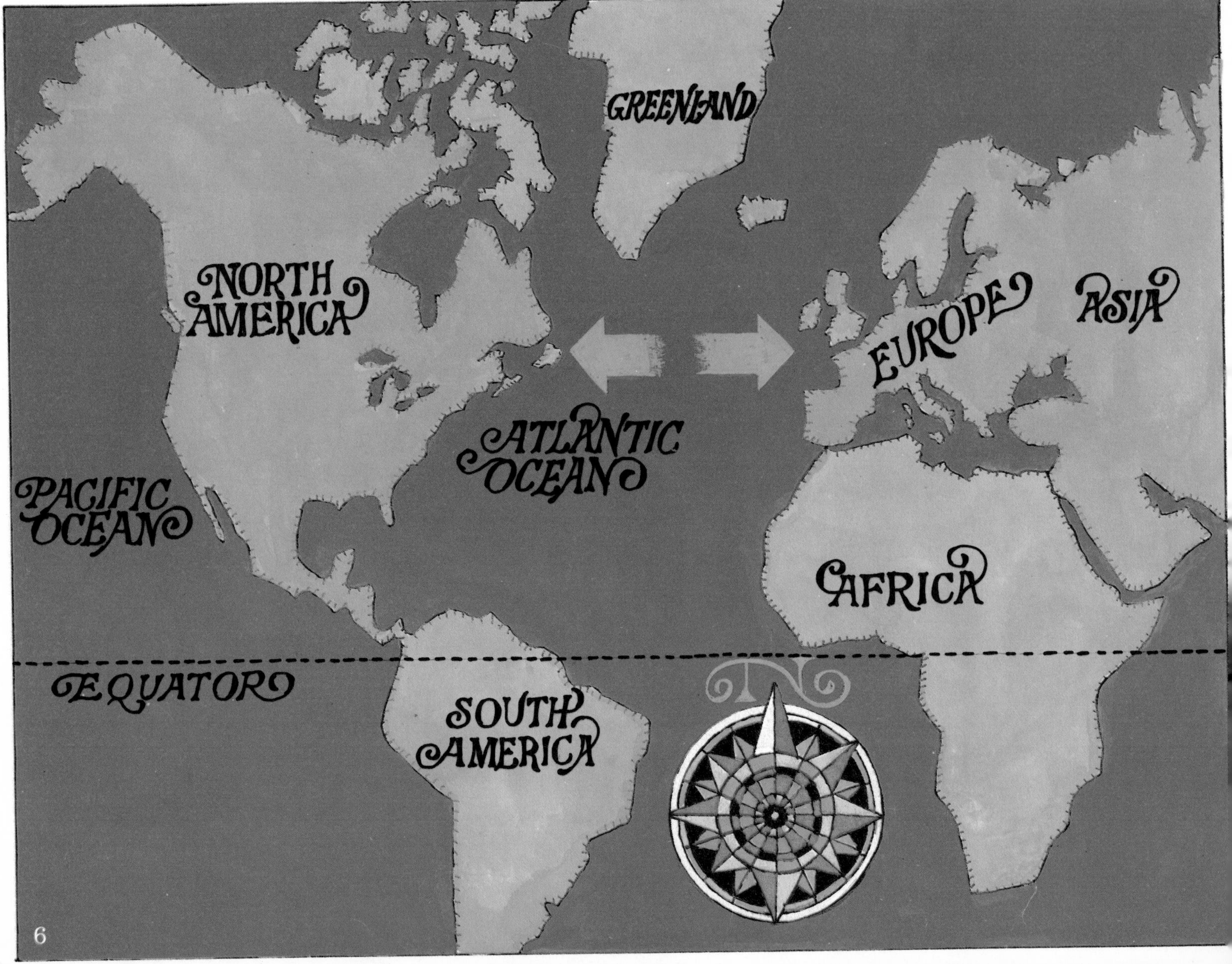

GREENLAND

NORTH AMERICA

EUROPE

ASIA

ATLANTIC OCEAN

PACIFIC OCEAN

AFRICA

EQUATOR

SOUTH AMERICA

6

Whole mountains move. Big sections of a continent like North America can move. Even whole continents move. Right now North America and Europe are moving apart. They move slowly, only as fast as your fingernails grow. So we don't feel the motion.

When parts of the Earth move quickly, there may be an earthquake. Every day there are at least a thousand earthquakes on our planet. Most are small, but each year there are a few earthquakes large enough to knock down buildings.

The strength of an earthquake can be measured. We use something called the Richter scale, named after C. F. Richter, an American scientist. Anything that measures less than 2 is a small quake, and 8 or higher is a very big one.

Every earthquake has a center. That's where it all begins. Parts of the Earth move up and down or sideways, and make waves that spread out and go through the whole Earth.

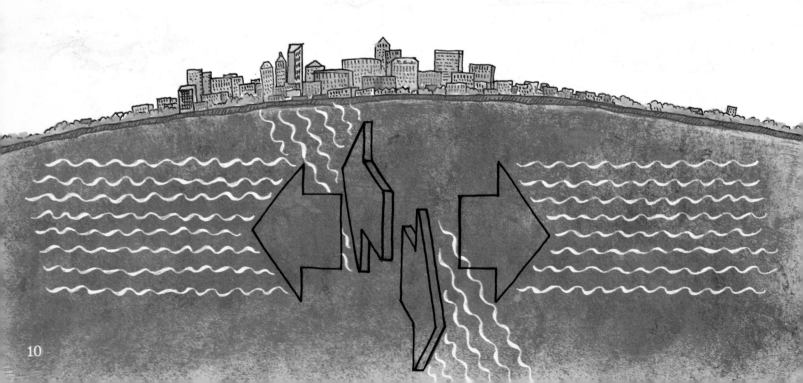

They are called seismic waves. The word comes from *seismos*, a Greek word meaning to shake. Scientists all over the world measure the waves on seismometers.

Here is an experiment to help you understand how waves work. Hold a yardstick near your ear. Have someone tap lightly on the other end. You can hear the sound clearly because a wave went through the yardstick. Waves travel through rock the way sound travels through wood.

There are also up-and-down waves, like the waves in a rope when you flip it up and down. This kind of wave also goes through the Earth.

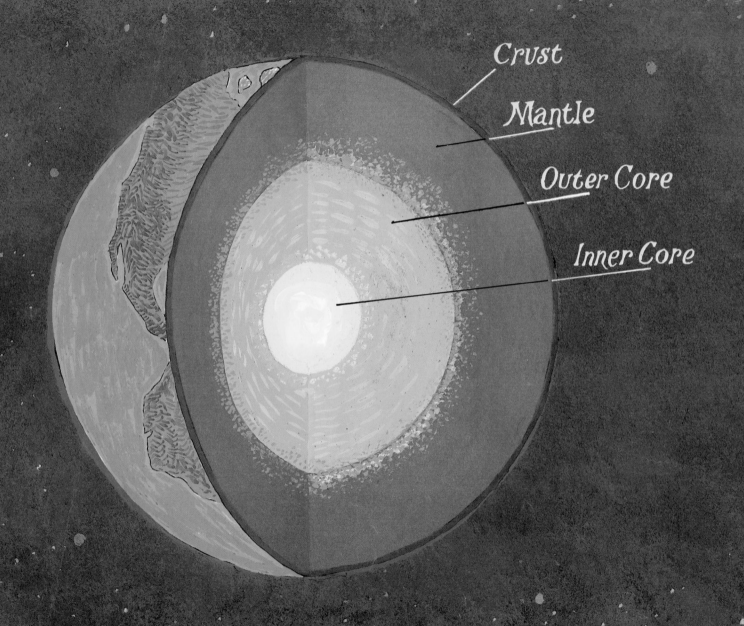

Crust

Mantle

Outer Core

Inner Core

We live on the outer part of Earth. It is called Earth's crust. In some places the crust is 30 or 40 miles thick. If Earth were an apple, the crust would be only as thick as the skin of the apple. Most earthquakes occur in the crust.

15

Large sections of the Earth's crust are always moving. Sometimes two sections push against each other. The place where they meet is called a fault. When the sections cannot pass, the earth bends and buckles. Suddenly the bend releases, and a whole section may move four or five feet at once. That's what happened twelve miles below the surface of Mexico in 1985. The seismic waves from the earthquake's center were strong enough to topple buildings in Mexico City, 220 miles away, and kill several thousand people. The quake measured 8.1 on the Richter scale.

Sometimes two sections of the crust scrape along-side each other. That makes a fault too. The San Andreas Fault is a crack in the Earth that runs north and south for hundreds of miles in California.

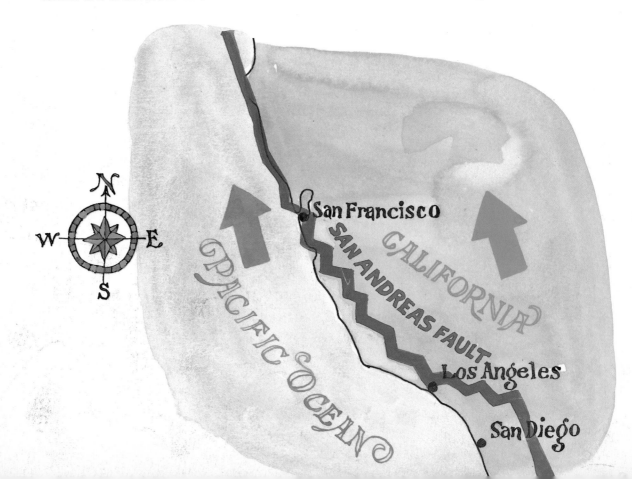

In 1906 there was an earthquake along a section of the San Andreas Fault. In seconds, the crust on the west side of the fault moved twenty feet. San Francisco and the area around the city shook and trembled. Fires started, and most of the city burned down.

Most earthquakes occur along the shores of the Pacific Ocean, where the crust moves a lot. Japan has about 7,000 quakes a year. Luckily, most are small.

There are volcanoes in this part of the world too. Earthquakes often occur in places where there are volcanoes. Melted rock deep under the Earth pushes upward, making the area shake and rumble. These are warnings that a volcano may erupt or that there may be a big earthquake.

In southern Europe there are several volcanoes. There are also many earthquakes. In Pozzuoli, Italy, a small town not far from Mount Vesuvius, there were 4,000 quakes in one year. Mount Vesuvius is a volcano that has erupted from time to time for several thousand years.

In 1939 a big fault opened up in the bottom of the sea, causing an earthquake just off the coast of Chile in South America. Water rushed into the opening. After it was filled, water kept rushing toward the fault. The water piled high, making a huge wave that traveled toward the shore. The wave was a wall of water called a tsunami, a Japanese word. People ran to the hills to escape, but a landslide caused by the quake swept them back into the sea. This was a big undersea earthquake.

In a small quake, dishes rattle. Ceiling lights swing. The ground jiggles a bit as if a big truck were going by. It's all over in a few seconds.

During a big earthquake, many buildings fall down. There are also fires. Pipes that carry gas to homes are broken. A spark may set the gas afire. Sometimes firefighters can't fight the flames because water pipes have broken.

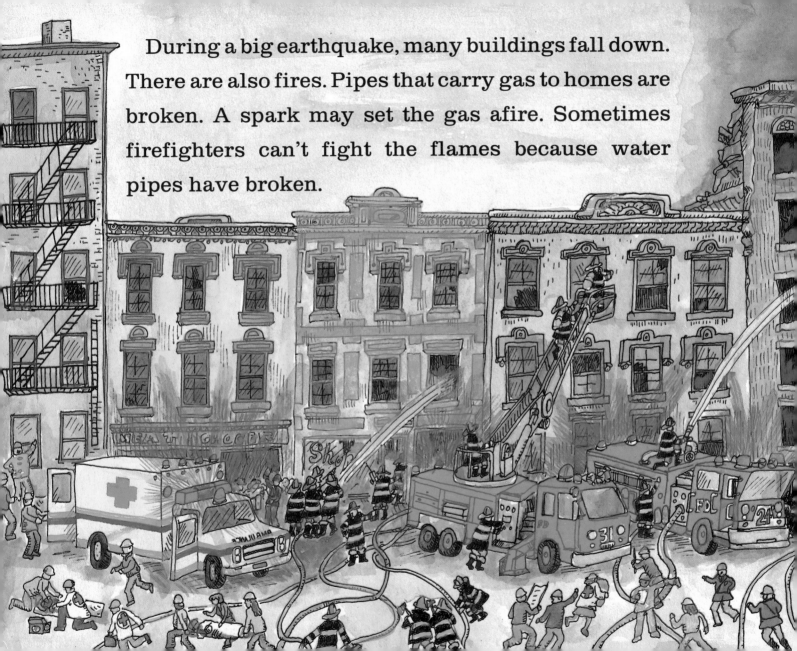

During an earthquake, dams may break too. Rivers may be blocked by landslides. So there is often flooding in the area of an earthquake.

In many parts of the world where there are big earthquakes, new buildings are made of steel instead of wood. They are built where the ground is solid so seismic waves will not knock them down. Old bridges and dams are made stronger with extra steel and concrete.

In 1989, there was a serious earthquake near San Francisco. It was the worst in the area since 1906. Sixty-seven people were killed. Bridges and roadways were damaged, and many buildings were destroyed. Because of the way it was built, the famous Golden Gate Bridge swayed in the quake, but it did not collapse.

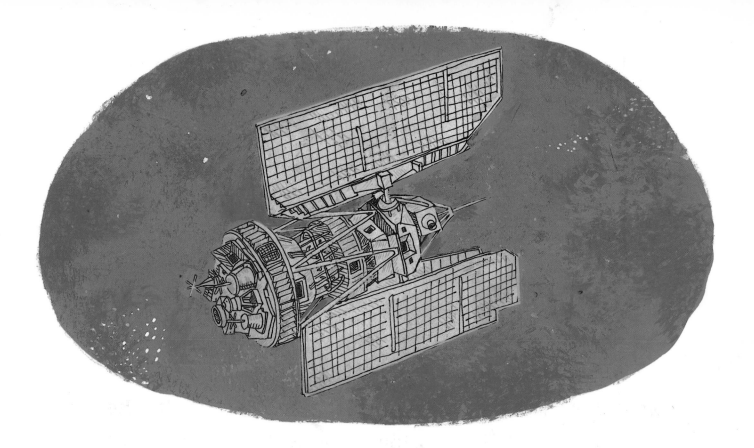

Earthquakes happen without any warning. However, scientists are working to find ways to predict quakes. They use satellites to measure even the smallest motion along faults. These small motions can often become larger.

It is important to know what to do in case of an earthquake.

If you are outside, stay away from buildings, trees, power lines, or anything else that could fall on you. If you can, go to an open space, like a ball field or parking lot.

If you are inside, stay there. Get under a strong table or bed, or stand in a doorway. Keep away from windows.

If you are in school, your teacher will tell you what to do.

Wherever you are, remember there may be smaller shocks after the main quake. These aftershocks could cause more damage.

People who live in places where there have been earthquakes should always keep a supply of plastic bottles of drinking water. They should also have a supply of canned food, a flashlight, a fire extinguisher, and a battery-powered radio.

The crust of our planet is always moving, so we will continue to have earthquakes. Most of them, fortunately, will be small ones.

We hope there is never a big earthquake near you. But if there is, you know there are things that you can do to protect yourself and other people.

Printed in Italy

A B C D E

Dad!
I can't sleep

Written and illustrated by

Michael Foreman

HARCOURT BRACE & COMPANY

San Diego   New York   London

Little Panda couldn't sleep.
"Mom!" he called. "Can I have a drink?"

Mom said, "It's your turn, Dad. I've done enough today."

Dad took little Panda a drink, kissed him goodnight,
and went downstairs.

"Dad!" called Little Panda. "I still can't sleep. Can I
 have another drink?"

"No," said Dad. "Go to sleep."

"I can't," said Little Panda.

"Count sheep," said Dad. "Then you'll go to sleep."

"How?" asked Little Panda.

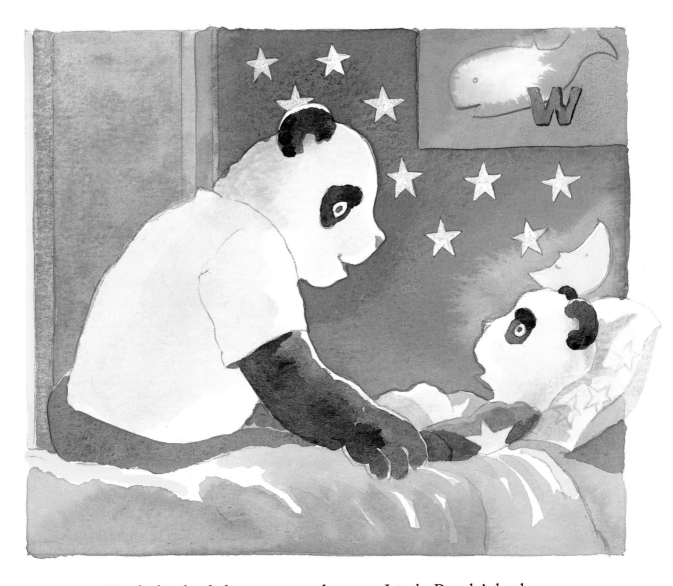

Dad climbed the stairs and sat on Little Panda's bed.
"How do I count sheep, Dad?" asked Little Panda.
"Just close your eyes," said Dad. "Now imagine sheep
jumping over a fence. Count them as they jump. One.
Two. Three. Four. Five. Six. Then you will fall asleep."

Little Panda closed his eyes and counted sheep.
"One. Two. Three. Four. Five and a lamb. Six.
Seven and another lamb. . . ."
Quietly, Dad went downstairs.

"Dad!" called Little Panda.
"I can't sleep."
"Count sheep!" called Dad.

"I've done that and I still can't
    sleep," called Little Panda.
"Count something else,"
    shouted Dad.
"Count cows!"

Little Panda closed his eyes and counted cows.
"One. Two. Three. Four. Five. Six. Seven.
Eight. Nine."
"Dad! I still can't sleep."

"I am not coming up again!" shouted Dad.
"Count pigs or tigers!"
  Little Panda counted tigers.
"Sixteen. Seventeen. Eighteen. Nineteen
  tigers and three little pigs."

"Dad! I still can't sleep."
"Count elephants — and I
don't want to hear from
you again!" shouted Dad.
Little Panda counted elephants.
"Forty-six. Forty-seven.
Forty-eight. Forty-nine."

Then he counted
rhinos and hippos,
giraffes and polar bears,
and still he couldn't sleep.
"Dad! I've counted all sorts
of things and I still can't sleep."

"Dinosaurs!" shouted Dad.
"Have you counted dinosaurs?"
"No," said Little Panda.
"Well, count dinosaurs. And you know
there are lots of different kinds. Make sure
you count all of them . . . AND GO TO SLEEP!"

Little Panda started to count dinosaurs.
"Two hundred and two diplodocuses. Two hundred and
three diplodocuses. Two hundred and four diplodocuses.
Forty-six stegosauruses. Forty-seven stegosauruses. . . ."

But still Little Panda couldn't sleep.
"Two zillion pterodactyls. Two zillion and one
pterodactyls. Two zillion and . . . Dad!"

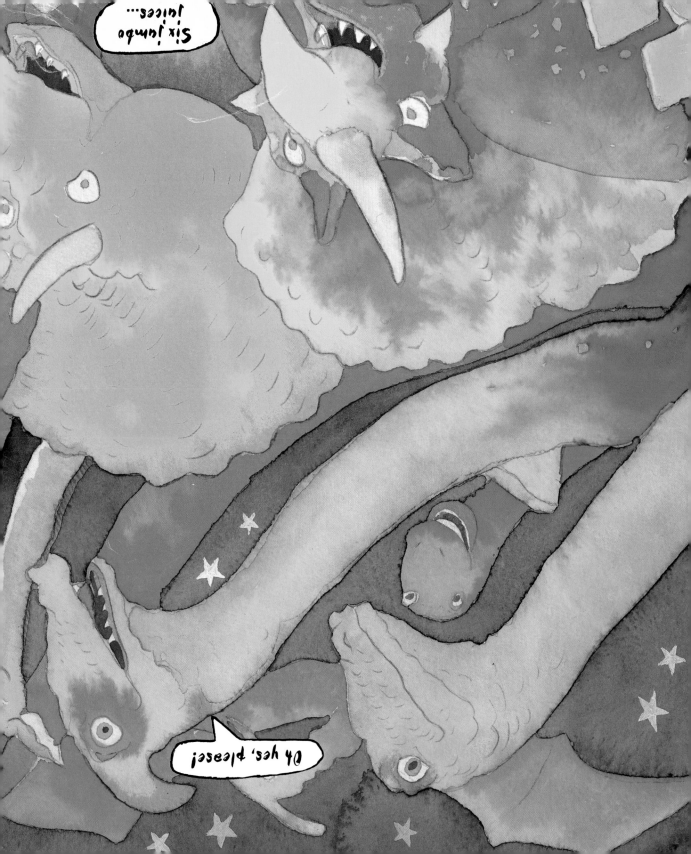

"Dad!"

"What is it now?" yelled Dad, and
he threw the laundry at the cat
and stamped up the stairs.

He pushed open Little Panda's door.